RAINBOW
ENGLISH PROGRAMME
1
FIRST CLASS BOOK

Rainbow English Programme for Prim

GW00372998

Getting Started!

Portfolio Book

CJ Fallon
ESTABLISHED 1895

MARIA REILLY

STAGE 2
BOOK 1

Published by
CJ Fallon
Ground Floor – Block B
Liffey Valley Office Campus
Dublin 22

ISBN: 978-0-7144-2866-6

First Edition April 2020

© Maria Reilly

Printed in Ireland by
W&G Baird Limited
Caulside Drive
Antrim BT41 2RS

Introduction

This ground-breaking **Portfolio book** accompanies the core book *Getting Started!* It reinforces the comprehension, vocabulary and other components covered in the core book. A unique feature of the portfolio book is that it covers all the **writing genres**. The portfolio is a clear record of the student's work for the year.

The Writing Genres

1. **Recount writing:** tells about the events in the order in which they happened. You can recount stories or events from storybooks, diaries, newspaper articles, history books and eye witness accounts.

2. **Report writing:** describes and gives clear information about objects, places, animals or people. You can make reports on newspaper articles, fiction or non-fiction books, games, meetings, races, a robbery, accidents, school sports day, parades and concerts.

3. **Explanatory writing:** explains how or why things occur. Examples of explanatory writing can be found in science books, on the internet, non-fiction books, SESE books or in encyclopedias.

4. **Narrative writing:** entertains and engages the reader in an imaginative experience. It includes the character(s), the setting and the event(s) leading to a problem and a solution to the same problem. Examples of narrative writing can be found in storybooks, novels, fairytales, fables, myths, legends, plays and poems.

5. **Persuasive writing:** is used to persuade others by involving argument and debate. Persuasive writing should have an introduction to the topic, a middle section discussing the topic in more depth and must finish with a final conclusion. Examples of persuasive writing are in debates, book and film reviews and advertisements.

6. **Writing to Socialise:** is used to maintain or enhance relationships. It can be formal or informal, depending on the relationship between the writer and the audience, e.g. postcards, letters, emails, texts, notes of apology, invitations and messages.

7. **Procedural writing:** contains a set of step-by-step instructions for doing something, e.g. a recipe or list of instructions for operating a machine, etc. Examples of procedural writing can be found in recipe and cookery books, assembly kits, rules for games, science books and maps.

8. **Free writing:** is used when you decide to use any genre of writing on any subject.

Contents

A Make a Gingerbread Person

Write the labels.

eyes	nose	mouth	arm	leg

My gingerbread person is called _____ .

B Fairy Tale Fun: Who am I?

Do you know these fairy tale characters?

| Three Little Pigs | Sleeping Beauty | Cinderella |
| Rapunzel | Goldilocks | The Big Bad Wolf |

Write the name of the fairy tale character.
Use these clues.

1. They built three houses. _____

2. She ate all the porridge. _____

3. He dressed up as granny! _____

4. She had a big sleep! _____

5. She threw down her long hair. _____

6. She did go to the ball. _____

1 The Gingerbread Boy

A **recount** tells what has happened. It sets the scene.

Setting the Scene

Who was there?	**When** it happened?	**Where** the event happened?

Read the story of *The Gingerbread Boy*. Set the scene.

Title: *The Gingerbread Boy*		
Who?	When?	Where?

What happened? Draw a picture.

4

D **Writing Genre: Recount Writing**

A **recount** tells what has happened. The events are told in order.

This is the story of Goldilocks.
Put the sentences in order.

The bears found Goldilocks.

The three bears came home.

Goldilocks ran home.

Goldilocks ate all the porridge.

2 Playground Games

Write true or false.

1. There are ten squares in hopscotch. _____

2. Three people hold the rope in skipping. _____

3. Mr Wolf kicks a football in the game. _____

4. Mr Wolf calls out *dinner time*. _____

5. Only girls can play hopscotch. _____

B **Time to Write**

Write about your favourite playground game.

Name of the game: _____

Draw a picture of the game.

© Writing Genre: Recount Writing

A **recount** tells what has happened. The events are in order.

Use **time words** to order a recount.

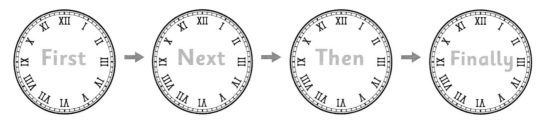

Write the recount in order. Use the pictures and time words to help you.

he was ready for the oven.	she made the gingerbread boy.
he jumped out of the oven.	he ran out the door.

First, _____

_____

Next, _____

_____

Then, _____

_____

Finally, _____

_____

D Writing Genre: Recount Writing

Read the story.

Yesterday, I was playing hopscotch in the playground at lunchtime. My friends Lucy and Emma were playing too. At first, we were having great fun. Next, Emma tripped and fell on the

ground. She hurt her knee.

Then, I asked our teacher for help. He cleaned Emma's knee and put a plaster on it. Finally, Emma felt better and came back to play.

Circle the time words in the story above.

First ➡ Next ➡ Then ➡ Finally

Now, answer the questions.

Where were the girls?	
Who was there?	
When did this happen?	
What happened?	

A Crossing the Road Safely

Fill in the spaces using these words.

listen	cross	look	don't cross
lollipop person	traffic light	zebra crossing	

1. What does this sign mean? _____

2. What does this sign mean? _____

3. Who is this? _____

4. What is this called? _____

5. What is this called? _____

6. Stop, _____, 👁 👁 and _____
   before you cross the road.

B Time to Write

Write three important things to remember when crossing the road.

1. _____

_____

2. _____

_____

3. _____

_____

Read your work.
Can you find one mistake?
Draw a circle
around it.

C Writing Genre: Recount Writing

A recount tells what has happened. It has a title.
It sets the scene. The events are in order.

Happy Birthday! Plan a recount of your birthday party.

Who was at the party?	**When** was the party?	**Where** was the party?
_____	_____	_____
_____	_____	_____
_____	_____	_____

What happened at the party?

_____

_____

_____

_____

_____

_____

_____

_____

_____

_____

_____

_____

_____

_____

D Writing Assessment: Free Writing 10 min

Free writing checklist ✓

		✓	
1.	Write whatever comes into your head.		
2.	Keep your pencil moving.		
3.	Don't use an eraser.		
4.	Work quietly. Do not disturb others.		

Colour a topic and write about it.

Autumn	Animals

Title:	Date:

A Wanted Poster!

Imagine you are the Witch.
Make a wanted poster for a new cat.

Checklist	
1. Must catch mice	✔
2. _____	☐
3. _____	☐
4. _____	☐

WANTED

B Time to Write

Write the note that the cat left for the Witch.

Dear Witch,

_____

_____

_____

_____

_____

_____

From _____

Read your work.
Can you find one mistake?
Draw a circle
around it.

ⓒ **Writing Genre: Narrative Writing**

A narrative tells a story. **Characters** are important. They are story stars!

Write about your favourite fairy tale character. Draw a picture. Write what they say.

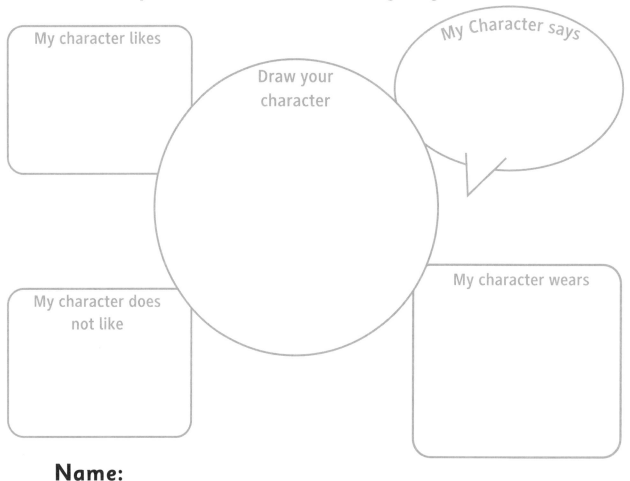

My character likes

My Character says

Draw your character

My character does not like

My character wears

Name: _____

Circle the correct word(s). My character is:

| good | naughty | kind | funny |

D Writing Genre: Narrative Writing

Characters are people, animals or creatures.
They are story stars. They can be good or bad!

1. The Witch is a story character**. Fill in her passport.**
Write what she might say.

EIRE / IRELAND / IRELANDE
PAS / PASSPORT / PASSEPORT

Name: _____

Appearance:

I have _____

I wear _____

More about me:

I like to _____

_____

_____

2. Colour the correct words to describe the character.

She is feeling:	**happy**	**sad**	**cross**	**lonely**
She is:	**good**	**bad**	**kind**	**busy**

A Colour Crossword

Write the colours. Fill in the crossword.

white	purple	red	yellow	blue
orange	green	pink	white	brown

ACROSS

3 _ _ _ _ _

5 _ _ _ _ _

7 _ _ _ _ _

9 _ _ _ _ _

DOWN

1 _ _ _ _ _ _

2 _ _ _ _ _

4 _ _ _

6 _ _ _ _

8 _ _ _ _

10 _ _ _ _ _ _

B Time to Write

Write a note to the crayons asking them to come back to work.

Dear Crayons,

_____

_____

_____

_____

_____

Your friend,

_____

Read your work.
Can you find one mistake?
Draw a circle
around it.

ⓒ **Writing Genre: Narrative Writing**

> A **narrative** tells a story.
> **Interesting words** make a story better.

1. Emoji Match

Read these interesting words.
Match them to the correct emoji.

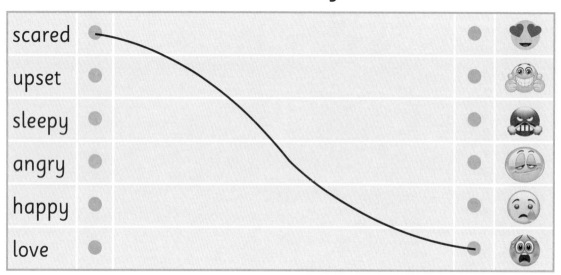

scared	
upset	
sleepy	
angry	
happy	
love	

2. Insert the correct words in the sentences below.

good	cross	like	tired	afraid

(a) I _____ eating chocolate cake.

(b) Dad was _____ with my older sister.

(c) I felt _____ after a busy day.

(d) My teacher is _____ of spiders.

(e) I had a _____ time at the party.

D Writing Genre: Narrative Writing

A **narrative** tells a story. A story has a beginning,
a middle and an ending.

Beginning	Middle	Ending
Set the scene. Who? Where? When?	Something happens in a story. This is an event. It leads to a problem.	The problem is resolved.

**Read the story *The Day the Crayons Quit*
Write the plan.**

Beginning	Middle	Ending
Who?	**The problem?**	**Resolution**
When?		Duncan uses all of his crayons to draw a special picture. The crayons are happy again.
Where?		

A **Hobbies**

1. Read the Hobbies. Match.

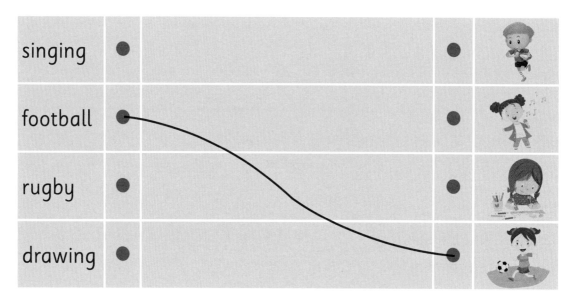

singing	●		●	
football	●		●	
rugby	●		●	
drawing	●		●	

2. Write about your hobbies.
  Draw a picture of your favourite hobby.

My Hobbies

My hobbies are _____

_____

My favourite hobby is _____

I like it because _____

I am good at _____

I need to work on _____

_____

B Time to Write

Write a note from Horrid Henry to his swimming teacher.

Dear Soggy Sid,

_____

_____

_____

_____

_____

From,
Horrid Henry

Read your work.
Can you find one mistake?
Draw a circle
around it.

C Writing Genre: Narrative Writing

Conjunctions are joining words. Use conjunctions
to join your words or sentences.

Read these conjunctions. **Use them to finish
the sentences.**

and	because	or	but	so

1. I went to the doctor _____ I was sick.

2. In winter he wears a coat, a hat _____ a scarf.

3. He spoke loudly _____ they didn't listen.

4. I was hungry _____ I made a sandwich.

5. Do you prefer the swimming pool _____ the cinema?

D Writing Assessment: Free Writing

Free writing checklist ✓

		✓	
1.	Write whatever comes into your head.		
2.	Keep your pencil moving.		
3.	Don't use an eraser.		
4.	Work quietly. Do not disturb others.		

Colour a topic and write about it.

My hobbies	Christmas

Title:	Date:

A **Christmas Presents**

1. Draw a picture of the best present you ever got.

The best present I ever got was a _____.

2. Draw a picture of the best present you ever gave.

The best present I ever gave was a _____.

B **Bossy Verbs**

Bossy verbs tell us what to do. They start a sentence.

Close the door.   Make your bed.

Write a bossy verb to finish each sentence.

Eat	Hang	Tidy
Brush	Play	Drink

1. _____your teeth carefully.

2. _____up your coat.

3. _____the glass of milk.

4. _____with your little sister.

5. _____your breakfast.

6. _____your bedroom.

7 The Girl and the Cloud

C Writing Genre: Procedural Writing

A **procedure** tells us how to do something. It has a title.
It lists the steps in order.

Write the sentences in order. Use the pictures to help.

Roll the cookie dough.	**Put** them in the oven.	**Put** icing on the cookies.
Let the cookies cool.	**Cut** the cookie shapes.	**Enjoy** eating the cookies.

Can you see the bossy verbs?

Title: How to make Christmas cookies.

1.	
2.	
3.	
4. Let	
5.	
6. Enjoy	

D **Writing Genre: Procedural Writing**

A **procedure** tells how to do something. It has a title.
It tells what you will need. It lists the steps in order.

Write about how to wrap a present.

Draw what you will need.

Title:
You will need:

scissors	sticky tape
wrapping paper	ribbon

Write the procedure.

1	Cut	
2	Wrap	
3	Stick	
4	Tie	

8 Timothy's Tooth

Ⓐ Crack the Code

A	B	C	D	E	F	G	H	I	J	K	L	M
9	17	2	14	7	22	24	11	25	18	3	19	12

N	O	P	Q	R	S	T	U	V	W	X	Y	Z
6	16	21	13	1	4	5	23	15	8	10	26	20

1. Now, Crack the Code!

5	11	7		5	16	16	5	11		22	9	25	1	26

__ __ __   __ __ __ __ __   __ __ __ __ __

2. Are these good ☺ for teeth or bad ☹ for teeth?

Draw the correct emoji beside them.

(a) juice	☹	(b) ice cream	
(c) toothpaste		(d) milk	
(e) sweets		(f) vegetables	
(g) apples		(h) cake	

B Time to Write

Imagine you are the Tooth Fairy collecting a tooth. Leave a thank you note for the child.

Dear _____

Thank you _____

_____

_____

_____

_____

_____

Love from,

_____

Read your work.
Can you find one mistake?
Draw a circle
around it.

31

C Writing Genre: Procedural Writing

Handwashing

Washing your hands is important. It keep germs away. Always wash your hands after using the bathroom and before you eat.

1 **First**, wet your hands.

2 **Next**, add a little soap. Rub the soap all over your hands.

3 **Then**, rinse the soap off your hands carefully.

4 **Finally**, dry your hands with a clean towel.

Now, write a procedure about how to wash your hands.

Title:	You will need:
	_____
	_____

Steps

1. Wet _____ _____	
2. Add _____ _____	
3. Rub _____ _____	
4. Rinse _____ _____	
5. Dry _____ _____	

D **Writing Genre: Procedural Writing**

Write a procedure about how to brush your teeth.

Title:	
You will need:	• Toothbrush • Toothpaste • Cup of water

HELPFUL BOSSY VERBS

Put   **Brush**
Move   Rinse

Steps

1. _____

2. _____

3. _____

4. _____

A Hidden Words

Read the clues. Unscramble the words.

1.	The Eurostar goes under the __ __ __.
2.	A famous steam engine. __ __ __ __ __ __
3.	A train runs on __ __ __ __ __ __.
4.	Famous television train. __ __ __ __ __
5.	Buy a __ __ __ __ __ __ for the train.
6.	A __ __ __ __ __ engine.

a e s

k t R o c e

t c r a k s

s T h m a o

e t c k i t

m s t e a

B Time to Write

Read the sentences. Cross out the extra word.

1. I put milk ~~salt~~ on my breakfast.

2. I went the on a train journey last week.

3. I bought a shop ticket for the train.

4. I travel walk to school on the bus.

5. I fell on off my bicycle and hurt my knee.

6. I missed lost my train home.

© **Writing Genre: Explanation Writing**

Explanations tell how something works.
The steps are in order.

How does a steam engine work?

Read the sentences. Write the correct numbers on the picture.

1.	Coal burns in the fire.
2.	The fire heats the water.
3.	The smoke goes up the chimney.
4.	The water turns into steam.
5.	The steam pushes the piston.
6.	The piston moves the wheels.

D Writing Assessment: Free Writing

Free writing checklist ✓

		✓	
1.	Write whatever comes into your head.		
2.	Keep your pencil moving.		
3.	Don't use an eraser.		
4.	Work quietly. Do not disturb others.		

Colour a topic and write about it.

The weekend	My family

Title:	Date:

A Help Salty get Home

Salty strayed from the island. Help him to find his way home to his mother.

B Time to Write

Imagine that you are Salty. Write a note to say sorry to the old bull.

Dear _____

_____

_____

_____

_____

_____

_____

From,

_____

Read your work.
Can you find one mistake?
Draw a circle
around it.

© **Writing Genre: Explanation Writing**

Fact or Fiction?

> Facts are true. They are real.

> Fiction is made up. It is not real.

1. Read the sentences. Write if they are fact or fiction.

1.	Clouds are made from cotton wool.	*fiction*
2.	Seals eat fish.	
3.	A young seal is called a pup.	
4.	Seals have arms and legs.	
5.	Seals use armbands to swim.	
6.	Seals have flippers.	

2. Read the sentences. Colour the one that is fact in blue. Colour the one that is fiction in red.

1. Suddenly, there was a puff of smoke. The wizard was gone. He had disappeared.
2. A mare is a female horse. Her babies are called foals.

D **Writing Genre: Explanation Writing**

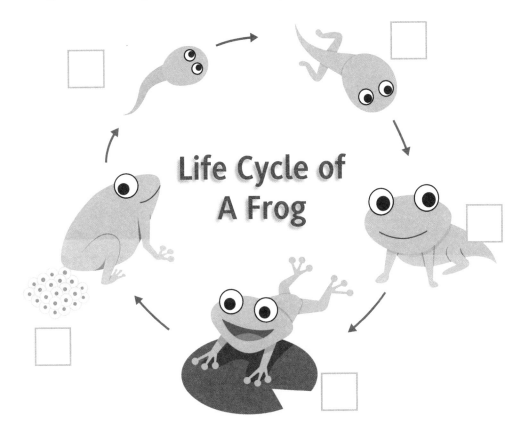

Life Cycle of A Frog

Match the number to the picture.

1	The frog lays eggs called frogspawn. Frogspawn looks like jelly.
2	After a week a baby frog called a tadpole hatches from the egg.
3	Next the tadpole grows two legs at the back.
4	The tadpole now has four legs and a shorter tail. It is called a froglet.
5	Finally the froglet becomes a frog.

A St Patrick's Day Parade

Design a poster for your school to carry in the St Patrick's Day Parade.

B Finish the Sentences

Tick the correct box to finish the sentences.

1	St Patrick's day is	on the 17th of March. ✔	at Christmas. ☐
2	Young Patrick looked after	ducks. ☐	sheep. ☐
3	God spoke to Patrick	on the telephone. ☐	in a dream. ☐
4	St Patrick spoke to the	High King. ☐	President. ☐
5	The druids were	wise men. ☐	Kings. ☐
6	Patrick explained about God using	a shamrock. ☐	a book. ☐

C Writing Genre: Narrative Writing (Poetry)

A rhyming couplet is two lines of poetry that rhyme at the end. **Rhyming words** sound similar.

1. Use the words to finish the rhyming couplets.

star	fall	red	tummy

Humpty Dumpty sat on a wall
Humpty Dumpty had a great
_____.

I got an egg from the Easter Bunny,
Now it's sitting in my
_____.

Twinkle, twinkle little _____,
How I wonder what you are.

Leaves of yellow,
brown and _____,
Falling down around my head.

2. Finish the second line. Use a rhyming word.

(a) There is something exciting about a **book**,
Open one and take a _____.

(b) He may seem friendly with his big **smile**,
But never trust a _____.

(c) When I was really young and **small**,
I couldn't walk, I could only _____.

(d) The weather is so nice **today**,
Let's all go outside and _____.

D Writing Genre: Narrative Writing (Poetry)

1. Circle the rhyming words in these couplets.

When I see the moon at night,	I went too fast on my skis,
It looks so beautiful and bright.	I fell and landed on my knees.

2. Use the rhyming words to write couplets about spring.

(a) I love to see the honey **bees**,	
_____ **trees**.	

(b) The season I like most is **spring**,	
_____ **sing**.	

(c) Today I saw a **butterfly**,	
_____ **sky**.	

(d) We run outside when we see the **sun**,	
_____ **fun**.	

A Name that Rabbit!

Use the wordbox to help you write the names.

Bugs Bunny	Easter Bunny	Thumper
	Snowball	Peter Rabbit	

1.	Carrot loving rabbit who says: _What's up doc?_	B__ __ __ B __ __ __ __
2.	Movie star rabbit from _The Secret Life of Pets._	S __ __ __ b __ __ l
3.	This bunny delivers eggs.	E __ __ t __ __ B __ __ __ __
4.	This rabbit steals from Mr McGregor's garden.	P __ __ __ r R __ __ __ __ __
5.	Friend of Bambi who thumps his foot.	T __ __ __ __ __ __

B Time to Write

Write a note thanking the Easter Bunny for your chocolate egg.

Dear Easter Bunny,

_____

_____

_____

_____

_____

_____

From,

_____

> Read your work.
> Can you find one mistake?
> Draw a circle
> around it.

C **Writing Genre: Narrative Writing (Poetry)**

1. Plan a poem about bunnies.
   Write rhyming words in the rhyming eggs.

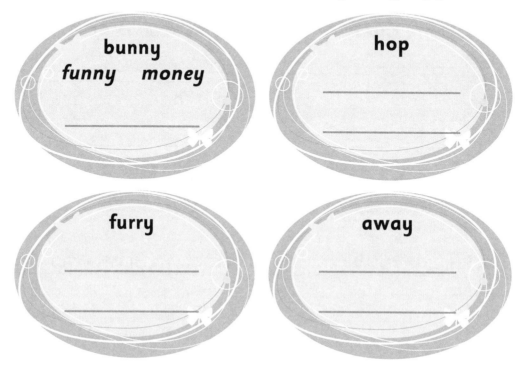

bunny
funny   money
_____

hop
_____
_____

furry
_____
_____

away
_____
_____

2. Give your poem a title. Use your plan to help you write the poem.

Title: _____

Line 1: _____

Line 2: _____

Line 3: _____

Line 4: _____

D Writing Assessment: Free Writing 10 min

Free writing checklist ✓

		✓	
1.	Write whatever comes into your head.		
2.	Keep your pencil moving.		
3.	Don't use an eraser.		
4.	Work quietly. Do not disturb others.		

Colour a topic and write about it.

The zoo	Easter

Title:	Date:

A Help the Dog!

Help the dog to find the bone.

B Dog Quiz

Colour the correct ending.

1.	A new born dog is called a	puppy	kitten	doggie
2.	Dogs are also called	cats	canines	insects
3.	Dogs feet are called	paws	claws	hands
4.	Dogs are very good at	smelling	driving	talking
5.	Dogs wag their tails if they are	happy	smelly	late
6.	Dogs are covered in	wool	hair	feathers
7.	Dogs should not eat	chocolate	dog food	meat

C Writing Genre: Report Writing

> Reports give information about something.
> They describe something.

Write words to describe the dog in the picture.

	_____
	_____
	_____
	_____
	_____

Use the words to write sentences about the dog.

1.	
2.	
3.	
4.	
5.	

Adjectives are describing words.

Read your work. Can you find one mistake? Draw a circle around it.

D Writing Genre: Report Writing

Title: Guide dogs

What is it? A special dog who helps and keeps their owner safe.

Where does it live? Guide dogs live with their owner. The owner can be an adult or a child.

What does it look like? Guide dogs are big dogs. They can be any colour. Guide dogs are often Labradors.

Fact 1: It takes two years to train a guide dog. They go to guide dog school to learn.

Fact 2: Guide dogs are very loyal. They work with their owner as a team.

Read and colour the parts of the report the correct colour.

Title ➡	**RED**
What is it? ➡	**YELLOW**
What does it look like? ➡	**GREEN**
Where does it live? ➡	**BLUE**
Fact 1 ➡	**PURPLE**
Fact 2 ➡	**PINK**

A Make a poster to help our bees in trouble.

Save the Bees

B Animal Homes

Write the home of each animal using the word box.

sea	warren	tree
pond	hive	den

1. A rabbit lives in a _____.

2. A honeybee lives in a _____.

3. A frog lives in a _____.

4. A bird lives in a _____.

5. A fox lives in a _____.

6. A seal lives in the _____.

C Writing Genre: Report Writing

1. What am I? Read the clues. Write and draw the answer.

(a)

I am an African animal.	**What am I?**
I eat leaves from the tree tops.	_____
I have a very long neck.	

(b)

I am a fruit.	**What am I?**
You can peel my skin.	_____
I am bendy and yellow.	

2. Look at the clock. Write three lines to describe what you see.

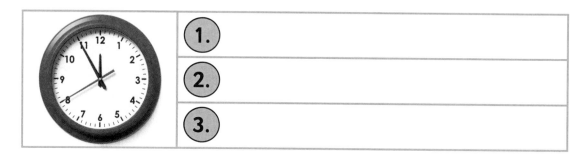

1.

2.

3.

D Writing Genre: Report Writing

Read the report about bees. Fill in the information.

Title:

What is it about?

What do they look like?   Where do they live?

Fact 1:   Fact 2:

A Your Teacher

Write about your teacher. Draw your teacher.

1. **My teacher's name is** _____.

2. **My teacher has** _____ **eyes.**

3. **My teacher likes** _____

   _____.

4. **My teacher says** _____

   _____.

5. **Sometimes my teacher** _____

   _____.

6. **My teacher is not** _____

   _____.

My teacher looks like this!

B People at Work

Unscramble the words. Write where the people work.

1.	A teacher works in a _____.	o o l s c h
2.	A nurse works in a _____.	h s p i t o a l
3.	A librarian works in a _____.	b r a r y i l
4.	A farmer works on a _____.	m r a f
5.	A chef works in a _____.	c h e n k i t
6.	A mechanic works in a _____.	a g e g a r

C **Writing Genre: Report Writing**

Read the report. Fill in the information.

Parrots

Parrots are colourful birds. They have strong legs and claws with four toes. They love to eat seeds. They use their beaks to crack them. Wild parrots live in hot areas. They live in flocks.

Parrots can live to be 100 years old. Parrots are clever. They have large brains. They can learn to use simple tools. Some parrots even copy what humans say. Parrots make good pets especially if you are a pirate!

Title:

What is it about?

What do they look like?

Where do they live?

Fact 1:

Fact 2:

D **Writing Assessment: Free Writing**

Free writing checklist ✓

		✓	
1.	Write whatever comes into your head.		
2.	Keep your pencil moving.		
3.	Don't use an eraser.		
4.	Work quietly. Do not disturb others.		

Colour a topic and write about it.

When I grow up	My favourite place

Title:	Date:

_____

_____

_____

_____

_____

Ⓐ Design a Medal

Design a medal that you would like to win.

My name: _____

Sport: _____

I won this medal for: _____

B **Agree or Disagree?**

Sometimes we agree with something and sometimes we disagree.

Write agree or disagree in the boxes below.

1.	Children should have PE every day.	
2.	All children should go to bed at 7 o'clock.	
3.	Boys are better than girls at sport.	
4.	Children should not have phones.	
5.	Children should have more homework.	
6.	School should stay open in the summer.	

Do you agree or disagree with Seán?

I _____ with Seán

because _____

_____

_____

_____

_____

Hi, I'm Seán. I love playing with my local GAA club. Every boy and girl should join their local GAA club.

Which is your favourite? Write the answer.

1. summer or winter

_____ is my favourite because _____

_____

2. cats or rabbits

_____ are my favourite because _____

_____

D Writing Genre: Persuasive Writing

Write what you like and dislike about school. Draw your school.

My School

Like 👍

Dislike 👎

A **Sports Day!**

1. List three Sports Day races.
Think of a funny new race to add to the list.

1. _____

2. _____

3. _____

My new race would be...

_____

_____

_____

2. Draw a picture of your race.

B **Hidden Sports!**

1. Read the list. Remove one letter to find the hidden sport.

a	s~~w~~wimming	*swimming*
b	horuse riding	
c	tenniss	
d	foootball	
e	runninng	

2. Match the sport to the picture.

hurling ● ●

hockey ● ●

basketball ● ●

rugby ● ●

© Writing Genre: Narrative Writing

Read the story.

Scooby on Sports Day

Mary and Sarah are twins. They live on a farm. Grandad Leo is very kind and nice. He bought them a donkey. They called him Scooby. Scooby loved to run.

Sports Day was coming. This year there was going to be a special race just for ponies. Sarah asked if donkeys could be in the race too and her teacher agreed.

Mary was worried. After all, Scooby was a donkey. Everybody knows that ponies are faster than donkeys. Each day after school the girls brought Scooby out to practise running. Scooby worked hard and he was good but the other ponies were bigger and faster.

Grandad Leo heard about the problem. He knew Scooby loved carrots. He thought of a plan. On sports day all the ponies were in a line ready to run. Little Scooby was there too but Mary and Sarah couldn't believe their eyes. There was a carrot tied to a stick in front of Scooby's nose.

Grandad knew that Scooby would run fast to try to catch the carrot. The teacher blew the whistle. The ponies were all very quick but Scooby was much quicker. He kept running to try to catch the carrot. Scooby won the race! Everybody cheered. The teacher gave Scooby a medal for first place. Sarah took the carrot off the stick and gave it to Scooby. Mary ran to Grandad Leo and gave him a big hug.

D Writing Genre: Narrative Writing

You have read the story of *Scooby on Sports Day.*
Now, write the plan.

Beginning	Middle	Ending

Who?

When?

Where?

The Problem?

The Resolution

A **Make a Checklist**

Write and draw what you need to bring on a sleepover.

1. _____

_____

2. _____

_____

3. _____

_____

4. _____

_____

B Write a Note

Imagine you are Hugo.
Write a note to Granny asking if you can stay.

Dear _____

May I _____

_____

_____

_____

_____

_____

_____

_____

Love,

_____

> Read your work.
> Can you find one mistake?
> Draw a circle
> around it.

Roll a dice. Write about the character that matches your number.

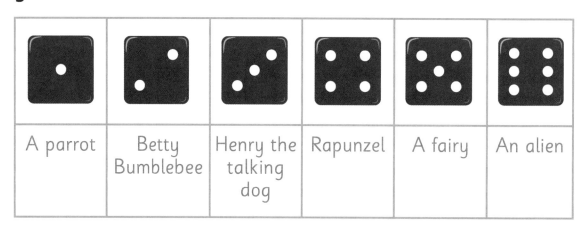

A parrot	Betty Bumblebee	Henry the talking dog	Rapunzel	A fairy	An alien

My character likes

My character looks like

My character says

My character does not like

My character wears

Name: _____

My character is _____

| good | evil | sad | funny |

D Writing Assessment: Free Writing 10 min

Free writing checklist ✓

		✓	
1.	Write whatever comes into your head.		
2.	Keep your pencil moving.		
3.	Don't use an eraser.		
4.	Work quietly. Do not disturb others.		

Colour a topic and write about it.

My School Tour	Summer holidays

Title:	Date:

_____

_____

_____

_____

_____

_____

NOTES

NOTES

NOTES